Excelling as a WOMAN

Titles in the School of the Word series:

A Life of Worship	John Johnson & Mike Stevens
According to Your Faith	Bryn Jones
Battle for the Mind	Stephen Matthew
Be Eager to Prophesy	Hugh Thompson
Called to be a Disciple	Dale Barnes
Christian Manhood	David Matthew
Effective Prayer	Bryn Jones
Essential Foundations	Hugh Thompson
Excelling as a Woman	Barbie Reynolds
Fulfilment in Marriage	Hugh & Rosemary Thompson
Getting the Most from the Bible	Stephen Matthew
Go and Make Disciples	Hugh Thompson
Issues Facing Society	John Houghton
Living in God's Security	Tony & Margaret Howson
Living in the Anointing	Paul Scanlon
Money Matters	Stephen Matthew
More Than Conquerors	Don Silber
Realities of the New Creation	Dale Barnes
Successful Parenthood	Hugh & Rosemary Thompson
Woman: Created for Success	Barbie Reynolds
Woman: Living in Victory	Barbie Reynolds

Excelling as a WOMAN

Barbie Reynolds

Harvestime

Published in the United Kingdom by:
Harvestime Publishing Ltd, 69 Main Street
Markfield, Leicester LE6 0UT, UK

ISBN 0-947714-05-7

Typeset in the United Kingdom by:
ScribeTech Ltd, Bradford BD8 7BX

Printed and bound in Great Britain by
BPCC Hazell Books
Aylesbury, Bucks, England
Member of BPCC Ltd.

Increasing numbers of people are wanting to study the Word of God in depth. To go to a Bible college or seminary is not feasible for the majority, yet they desire more than the average church is able to provide in its teaching curriculum.

The book you are about to study is part of a library of components that together provide a comprehensive overview of the Scriptures in relation to life. Each book is complete in itself but is developed in such a way that the best result is experienced by studying it as part of the whole series.

We have produced the curriculum so that each component, in addition to its use as a personal study, can provide a seven-week teaching programme for study in church, home, college campus, school, military base, prison or any other group setting.

It is our prayer that you will be greatly enriched in your spiritual development through this book.

Bryn Jones
Founder — School of the Word

Getting the Most Out of This Study

This School of the Word study book is one of a series designed to relate Bible truths to everyday life. Each of the seven lessons starts with a direct search of the Scriptures and ends with a challenge to the student to apply the truths discovered. As the blank spaces left in Bible verses are filled in, the most important words and phrases stand out clearly on the page.

The material can be used in a number of different ways. It can form the basis of an individual study or be used in a group setting over a number of weeks. But experience has shown that it has the greatest benefit when a group of people study it together under a leader who is well prepared.

Tips for Leaders

If you are a leader planning to take a number of people through this study, you should consider the following:

1. Be prepared

It is essential that you do the whole study in advance yourself. This will help you to be conversant with the basic outline and have a feeling for the level of teaching based on it that your students can take.

2. Keep to the outline

It is important to keep to the outline contained in this study. This has been carefully designed to build principle on principle, 'precept upon precept' (Isaiah 28:10 RAV), with the eventual aim of the student becoming 'thoroughly equipped for every good work' (2 Timothy 3:17).

Whatever happens, don't allow your teaching to digress and become an opportunity to preach an hour's sermon!

3. Use your own experience

Even though you are staying with the outline, where possible introduce additional illustrations and applications drawn from your own experience. This makes the basic teaching more relevant to the local setting. In addition, you may wish to add more emphasis to certain points.

4. Avoid indigestion

Each lesson should take about an hour to complete. You may like to divide this into two half-hour sessions by arranging a short break for coffee and a chat halfway through. That way, the teaching is kept to manageable portions.

In some cases you may feel that the group discussion is of such vital importance to your local area that you want to spread each lesson over two weeks. If you do this, try to divide the questions at the end so that they are relevant to that week's teaching.

5. Have the right tools

Make sure that all the students have access to a copy of the New International Version of the Bible — upon which the book is based. Encourage them to fill in the blank spaces in advance but to leave answering the true/false questions until after each teaching session.

Tips for Students

Before you start the study you need to ask yourself: Am I really committed to growing as a disciple of Jesus Christ? If the answer is yes, then you're ready to proceed. Here are some immediate steps you can take to ensure maximum benefit from the course:

1. Determine your goal

This book is designed to help you achieve God's goal and destiny for you. It doesn't matter whether you are young or old, a recent convert or someone who has been a Christian for many years.

Today you are taking a step towards the fulfilment of your destiny.

Look ahead and see yourself as God desires you to be. Then confess your commitment: 'This is the kind of person I *will* become.'

2. Plan your progress

Your faith commitment to work through this book, and so take one more step towards becoming the person God intends you to be, must not only be pursued but measured in its progress. The apostle Paul said:

> 'By the grace given me I say to every one of you: Do not think of yourself more highly than you ought, but rather think of yourself with sober judgment, in accordance with the measure of faith God has given you.'
>
> (Romans 12:3)

You know the kind of person you already are. You know the level of commitment you already have in your life. Now from this point determine how much time per day or week you are prepared to give to the study of the Word of God to achieve your goal.

At the end of each lesson in this study-book there is an opportunity for you to complete assignments and answer some Bible-based questions. This helps to fix the Word of God more firmly in your heart, and thus provide a reservoir of truth that the Holy Spirit can draw upon in the training of your life.

3. Recruit to the study course

Fellowship is one of the keys to Christian growth. The word 'fellowship' comes from the Greek word *koinonia*, which means to 'share things in common'.

Nothing will facilitate your progress as much as encouraging others to share in the same study programme with you, either on a personal basis or in a group. Share with each other the things you are learning and discovering in the Word of God and in life.

In this way you will be able to practise together much of what you study, and so strengthen each other in faith, just as 'iron sharpens iron' (Proverbs 27:17).

4. Set and maintain your standards

If this study is to be of maximum benefit to you, it must not be hurried. It is no use merely reading the written material and rushing the assignment. The book is designed to provoke you to your own searching and thinking, and to a demonstration of faith in God.

5. Check your progress

Once you have worked right through the book, ask your pastor or church leader to read through your answers. If he is satisfied that you have done your best to complete the questions, get him to send us a note to this effect. We will then forward a certificate for him to sign and present to you.

Your pastor is also the best person to monitor your progress and share your zeal to develop as a Christian disciple. If you are at college, university or in the armed forces, or for some other reason have no immediate access to a pastor, send us your book enclosing return postage and we will send it back to you with your certificate.

School of the Word
Harvestime Publishing Ltd
69 Main Street
Markfield
Leicester LE6 0UT
UK

Contents

Unless otherwise stated, Scripture quotations are taken from the New International Version.

Other versions referred to in this series include the New American Standard Bible (NASB), the Revised Authorised Version (RAV) and the Amplified Bible (Amp).

Verses have blank spaces for you to insert the missing words as you follow the Scriptures. This will deepen the impact of the Bible in your life.

A Woman of Dignity

1. Introduction

God created humankind in his image, 'male and female he created them' (Genesis 1:26-27). God's nature has many facets, and woman uniquely expresses one of them. She is *not* an afterthought, only here to meet man's need of a helper and companion. She is here because God has sovereignly chosen her to express a part of his nature and reflect qualities of his character that man cannot. God's delight and pleasure is in each woman he has created.

The book of Proverbs is full of practical advice for everyday living. Proverbs 31:10 (NASB) asks, 'An excellent wife, who can find?' The passage that follows implies that such a woman commands respect from her children, is praised by her husband, is praised by others and is valued and honoured in the community. What is her secret?

> 'Many women do noble things, but you **surpass them all**.'

> (Proverbs 31:29)

Other women previously recorded in the Bible include: Deborah, a military adviser; Miriam, who led a nation's women in praise to God; Huldah, who revealed God's plan to national leaders; Ruth, an example of covenant relationships; Hannah, the ideal mother; the Shunammite woman, who was known for her hospitality; Esther, who risked her life to save God's people; and Sarah, a woman of faith. Yet the woman who excels them all is the one who reverently and worshipfully 'fears the Lord' (Proverbs 31:30). Her spiritual and practical devotion to God permeates every area of her life.

God's power within us has given us everything we need to live a godly life (2 Peter 1:3). It is God's will for us to have the same nature and spirit that Jesus had. For this reason, we are to give ourselves diligently to goodness [moral excellence], knowledge, self-control, perseverance, godliness, brotherly kindness and Christian love (2 Peter 1:5-7). If these qualities are ours and are increasing, we will not be useless but fruitful in our knowledge of Jesus. And as long as we practise them, we will not stumble.

These same qualities are mentioned in Proverbs with particular reference to women. Each woman God has made has a unique personality. Each is an example of God's creativity. This series of studies looks in detail at different qualities that characterise a woman seeking to express God's heart and nature in her life. They aren't 'just for singles' or 'only for married women'. The Holy Spirit will apply them to the daily life of *any* woman who is seeking after Jesus with all her heart.

God wants to express these qualities increasingly through each unique woman. God will change you, not by applying a standard to your life for you to try to achieve, but by the Holy Spirit's working in and through you for his glory and pleasure as you daily respond in love and obedience to him. As each quality becomes yours and is increasing, you will be both useful and fruitful in your knowledge of Jesus — and so you will express his very nature.

2. Clothed with Dignity

What does the word *dignity* mean to you? 'Aloofness' perhaps? An air of superiority? Visions of the Royal Family? None of these describes the woman of Proverbs 31, whose worth is far above rubies (v10). Two of the meanings of the word *dignity* given in the Oxford English Dictionary are 'self-respecting' and 'worthy'. In Proverbs 31:25 we read that this woman has clothed herself with dignity. She has put on her self-respect and lives her whole life in a manner worthy of her position and calling.

A Woman of Dignity

Do you know your worth? Does *your* life speak of the dignity of your calling?

Insert your own name in the blanks:

> *'God so loved* _______________________ ___________________
> *that he gave his one and only Son, that [since]*
> _________________ *believes in him [she] shall not perish*
> *but have eternal life.'*
>
> (John 3:16)

To God, you are worth his own Son, Jesus. What higher calling can there be than to be a joint heir with the Son of God?

To become a woman of dignity, a woman who knows and expresses her self-worth, you must:

☐ Take off your old ways.

☐ Believe that God accepts and enjoys you.

☐ Begin in practical ways to clothe yourself with dignity.

3. Take Off Your Old Ways

Scripture talks a lot about clothing:

> *'All of you who were baptised into Christ have*
> _____________ __________________ *with Christ.'*
>
> (Galatians 3:27)

> *'* _____________ __________________ *with humility towards*
> *one another.'*
>
> (1 Peter 5:5)

> *'Awake, awake, O Zion, clothe yourself with strength.*
> *______ ____ your ______________ ____ ____________ , O*
> *Jerusalem, the holy city.'*
>
> (Isaiah 52:1)

Before we can clothe ourselves with dignity, we must first discard every negative attitude of mind that has robbed us of our feelings of self-worth:

> *'Do not conform any longer to the pattern of this world,*
> *but be ___________________ by the _______________*
> *of your mind.'*
>
> (Romans 12:2)

Many women carry negative feelings and are so weighed down by the pressures of life that they can't begin to put on the self-respect and dignity God intends for them. They need to be transformed by the renewing of their mind.

Common factors for many women are:

a. Self-rejection and feelings of inferiority

'I just can't cope like other women seem to.' 'I feel such a failure with the children.' 'I know I'll never get married; no man will ever want me.' These and hundreds of other similar thoughts eat away inside many women. Reasons for negative feelings about ourselves include:

☐ Rejection and abuse from parents (physical, emotional or sexual).

☐ Ridicule as a child from teachers, family or friends.

☐ Believing Satan's lies: 'You're a failure.' 'Everyone knows you're no good.' 'You'll never make it.'

☐ Salvation by 'works'. Trying to earn God's favour produces constant condemnation and feelings of worthlessness.

b. Insecurity in their relationship with God

'I can't feel God's love for me.' 'I've made such a mess of my life, God can't use me.' 'I'm not really important and, anyway, I'm just stuck at home with the children — that's enough, isn't it?' 'I'm not married, so there isn't anything of real significance I can do in the church.'

Left unchecked, these negative feelings and attitudes can have serious consequences. Insecurity and rejection eventually lead to bitterness towards God, the feeling that he's responsible and therefore can't be trusted. Negative feelings result in a resistance to authority and bitterness towards parents, husband, government or church leaders. They produce the belief that God is somehow depriving you.

Feeling deprived causes some women to strive for things God hasn't planned for them. Their insecurity causes them to over-emphasise material things or even spiritual gifts to compensate for the lack of inner rest and security in God. Others become preoccupied with themselves and their own needs. As a result, genuine friendships and relationships are stifled.

But the *truth* is:

> ' *"I know the plans I have for you," declares the Lord,*
> *"plans to _____________ you and not to harm you, plans*
> *to give you ________ and a _____________ ."* '
>
> (Jeremiah 29:11)

Jesus died to free us from rejection, inferiority and insecurity. He came to give us a new start with a new dignity.

4. How to Take Off the 'Old Clothing'

Repent of sinful, negative attitudes that make and keep you insecure. Deliberately renounce any of the following, or any other sinful attitude or practice that you know is holding you back from the dignity of your calling as a child of God:

a. Self-rejection

'I'm just no good. I'm not capable like other women.' 'My sister got all the brains and the looks in our family.'

> *'Who are you, [O woman], to talk back to God? "Shall what is formed say to him who formed it, 'Why did you make me like this?' " '*
>
> (Romans 9:20)

Self-rejection is closely bound to self-pity, which in turn leads to discouragement, depression and a complaining spirit. In Deuteronomy 28:47-48 we are told of the seriousness of not serving the Lord with a joyful heart.

b. Jealousy, envy, striving

'What has *she* done to deserve a lovely house like that, when we only have a two-bedroomed apartment?' 'She's always being asked out by different guys. She's just a flirt!' 'She can speak so confidently. They always ask *her* to do things in the church. They're just not spiritual enough to recognise *my* gift.'

Jealousy and envy in the heart will prevent you from forming close, deep relationships with other women. They will also stop you from knowing your own self-worth.

> *'Does not the potter have the right to make out of the same lump of clay some pottery for noble purposes and some for common use?'*
>
> (Romans 9:21)

c. Self-righteousness

Some of the results of trying to merit God's favour by outward practices are:

☐ Outward submission, false smiles and 'nice' talk.

☐ An immaculate house to 'prove' you are a good wife.

☐ Seeking to exercise more and more spiritual gifts in the meeting to show how 'spiritual' you are.

Ask God's forgiveness and pray, 'Jesus, take me as I am. I can come no other way.' On what basis are we acceptable to God?

> *'It is by _____________ you have been saved, through faith — and this _____ _________ ________________ , it is the _________ of God — not by works, so that no-one can boast.'*

(Ephesians 2:8-9)

5. Believe that God Accepts and Enjoys You

God loves you just as you are. He accepts you no matter what you do or don't do. There is nothing you can do to merit his love. Jesus took the complete penalty for our failure and sin, so, if you are in Christ Jesus, God no longer holds anything against you. He doesn't hold your failure against you and he loves you without any credentials. He has hand-picked you, not for what you can produce, but because you are precious enough for him to have given his own Son to die for. Hallelujah!

'Very rarely will anyone die for a righteous man, though for a good man someone might possibly dare to die. But God demonstrates his own love for us in this: _________ ____ _________ _________ _____________ , Christ died for us.'

(Romans 5:7-8)

☐ No-one else is worth more to God than you.

☐ No-one else is more loved by God than you.

☐ Your life is as potentially effective and powerful for God as anyone else's life.

'It is God who works in you to will and to act according to his good purpose.'

(Philippians 2:13)

If this is how God sees you, you have no right to reject yourself. You are not your own any more; you have given away your right to yourself and have become the King's daughter. If he says you are precious and lovely, you had better not contradict him!

6. Clothe Yourself with Dignity

We can learn a lot from the Bible book of Esther. Esther was an orphan, brought up by her cousin, Mordecai, who himself was a prisoner of war, exiled from Jerusalem. She had never known what it was to live as a free woman in her own land and among her own people. Yet she was chosen by the king of Persia to be queen over the most powerful and influential kingdom of her time.

'The king gave a great banquet, Esther's banquet, for all his nobles and officials. He proclaimed a holiday throughout the provinces and distributed gifts with royal liberality.'

(Esther 2:18)

Did Esther say, 'Oh, but I'm not worthy — I'm only an orphan. I'm bound to put my foot in it,' or, 'It's just not "me" to be royalty'?

No. *God chose* Esther to be queen, *for his purposes*. Esther responded to God's call on her life, not because she was naturally qualified, but because:

a. She had a submissive heart towards those God had put over her

> *'She asked for nothing other than what Hegai, the king's eunuch who was in charge of the harem, suggested. And Esther won the favour of everyone who saw her.'*
>
> (Esther 2:15)

Even when, strictly speaking, she was not obliged to take Mordecai's advice, her response to him shows her submissive heart and attitude:

> *'Esther had kept secret her family background and nationality just as Mordecai had told her to do, for she continued to follow Mordecai's instructions as she had done when he was bringing her up.'*
>
> (Esther 2:20)

Our submissive, loving response to what God says about us and his view of us causes us to rise up in the true dignity of our calling. We will no longer say negative things about ourselves. 'I'm a hopeless mother' will turn to, 'God is helping me to become the best mother my children could possibly have.' 'I'm just so unattractive — if only I could lose weight' will turn to, 'I'm beautiful to God and I'm going to explore ways of letting that inner beauty show on the outside. God's going to help me express his love of beauty through the way I take care of myself, my appearance and my eating habits. I'll love myself because God loves me.'

b. She wasn't afraid to face difficult situations

When faced with a crisis — for example, a child is hurt, or carefully made plans have been drastically upset — women are prone to rush ahead, jump to conclusions and take things into their own hands. Not so with Esther.

With the possible annihilation of the Jews at stake, Esther risked her life to petition the king on their behalf. She didn't rush into anything in a panic; she waited for God's timing and clear direction, and then, fully facing the possible consequences, she did what she knew she must do:

> *'I and my maids will fast as you do. When this is done, I will go to the king, even though it is against the law. And if I perish, I perish.'*
>
> (Esther 4:16)

As we appreciate our self-worth more and more, growing in our response to what God says about us, we will be able to succeed in every crisis. We will no longer shrink back, feeling that we aren't equipped to be the kind of woman God is calling for.

> *'I can do _______________________ through him who gives me _______________ .'*
>
> (Philippians 4:13)

c. She knew what God had called her to do

Many women fail to live in the dignity of their calling as daughters of the King because they constantly compare themselves with others. Their frame of reference is not, 'Am I fulfilling what God is calling me to do at this time?' but, 'How am I matching up to what other women around me are doing?'

God prospered and blessed Esther in every way as she fulfilled her God-given task. Those whom she loved also received the overflow of God's blessing on her life:

> *'Mordecai was prominent in the palace; his reputation spread throughout the provinces, and he became more and more powerful.'*
>
> (Esther 9:4)

We, too, can expect to see the positive effect of God's grace working on those who are dear to us, as we respond to God.

There came a day when the king promoted Esther to rule over part of his kingdom. But she wasn't pressured to take on more than God was giving her to do. She was easily able to hand on to others those things that were over and above what God had called her to:

> *'That same day King Xerxes gave Queen Esther the estate of Haman, the enemy of the Jews. And Mordecai came into the presence of the king, for Esther had told how he was related to her. The king took off his signet ring, which he had reclaimed from Haman, and presented it to Mordecai. And Esther appointed him over Haman's estate.'*
>
> (Esther 8:1-2)

We, too, need to be very clear at any given time as to our priorities and what it is that God is expecting of us. Then we will not be pressured by others' expectations or a sense of failure at not meeting conflicting demands. As daughters of the King of kings we will live in a worthy manner, fully expressing our own self-respect.

* *

LESSON 1

A Woman of Dignity

True or False

1. T F All Christian women are already dignified.

2. T F How we feel about ourselves affects our response to God.

3. T F God's word about us is only effective if we believe it and align our behaviour with it.

4. T F Some people are called to be more effective than others.

5. T F Dignity is an attitude of aloofness.

6. T F Each of us is chosen by God because of what we can do for him.

7. T F Our usefulness to God is not limited by the circumstances of our birth and upbringing.

8. T F We should always act immediately we see a need.

9. T F As we become dignified women of God we will feel superior to other women.

10. T F To become dignified is optional in our walk with God.

Group Discussion

1. What is the difference between being 'clothed with strength and dignity' (Proverbs 31:25) and thinking of yourself 'more highly than you ought' (Romans 12:3)?

2. What qualities command your respect in older women?

3. What qualities command your respect in younger women?

4. Consider a wife with young children. Identify the pressure areas that undermine her dignity (her feelings of self-worth and self-respect). How would you help her? Identify other stages of womanhood that come under pressure, and consider what help can be given.

Personal Assignment

1. If you have not already done so, repent specifically of any negative attitude that is preventing you from being 'clothed with strength and dignity' (Proverbs 31:25).

2. Consider prayerfully how you express your dignity as a child of God in the following areas:

   a. The way you look after yourself, for example, the way you dress, the food you eat, the sleep you have and your personal hygiene.

   b. The way you speak about yourself.

3. Identify the two areas where you most need to 'put on' dignity in your own life. What are you going to do about them?

True of False

1.F 2.T 3.T 4.F 5.F 6.F 7.T 8.F 9.F 10.F

The Wise Woman Builds Her House

'The wise woman builds her house, but with her own hands the foolish one tears hers down.'

(Proverbs 14:1)

Definitions:

Wise = 'Having judgment and the power of discerning or evaluating what is right or wrong, reasonable, etc' (Webster's Universal Dictionary).

'The fear of the Lord is the beginning of knowledge.'

(Proverbs 1:7)

House = 'A building for dwelling in, household affairs, a family, kindred.' (Oxford Dictionary)

Build = 'Construct or erect by successive additions (house, nest, empire, reputation).' (Oxford Dictionary)

1. Introduction

A woman who wants to please the Lord is wise. She will build, by successive additions, a life that is pleasing to God. She will diligently construct a lifestyle in which her household affairs and relationships in her family — including the wider family of God, of which she is part — bring pleasure and delight to God's heart.

Can you imagine a builder starting to put up a house without first looking at the blueprint, or knowing exactly what type of house he was going to build? When asked what he was building, his reply would be, 'I don't know. I'm just building.'

The idea is absurd. Yet many women live their lives that way. They take each day, week and year as it comes — piles of washing, loads of dishes, cleaning, meals to prepare, a job to hold down, church meetings to attend, children to raise. They are just building.

When the pressure mounts up and the storms come, they are filled with negative, despairing thoughts; everything within them rebels against the treadmill. In Scripture, 'foolish' means rebellious. The foolish woman tears down her house with her own hands. A woman can destroy the very things God has given her to build, simply because she doesn't have a clear idea what she is building.

Remember:

☐ God has a blueprint for your life.

☐ God wants you to build with purpose each area of your life.

☐ If you fear the Lord in its proper sense you will be willing to change your way of running your life and your home to a way that honours him.

What about the single woman?

> *'An unmarried woman or virgin is concerned about the _____________ ____________ : Her aim is to be ______________ to the Lord in both _________ and __________ .'*
>
> (1 Corinthians 7:34)

The single woman who loves the Lord is single for the kingdom of God. She is not single merely because she isn't yet married. She has a 'house' to build for God — her whole life is given to serving the Lord.

Her secular employment:

☐ Provides an income to support herself and to give away.

☐ Is a means of involvement in and serving the community at large.

☐ Is a training ground for producing godly character.

The single woman has the same opportunity to fulfil the call of God on her life as does any married woman. There is nothing that God has purposed for her, at this present time, that being single bars her from:

> *'No _________ thing does he withhold from those whose walk is _____________________ .'*
>
> (Psalm 84:11)

If you walk with God and he sees that marriage would be a good thing for you and that it would increase your fruitfulness for him, he won't withhold it. If he sees that marriage (or anything else) would not be a good thing for you, then — praise God — he'll withhold it from you!

2. The Foundation

> *'Let us leave the elementary teachings about Christ and go on to maturity, not laying again the foundation of _____________________ from acts that lead to death, and of _________ ____ _______ .'*
>
> (Hebrews 6:1)

The foundation, as we saw in lesson 1, is knowing our self-worth, repenting of dead actions and having faith in God:

☐ Secure in God's love.

☐ Certain that you are forgiven, chosen, loved and cared for by God.

☐ Knowing who you are — God's beloved daughter.

3. Building Relationships

Women have many roles. It is important to accept these ever-changing roles from God and to repent of any envy you have of others' roles. Envy will destroy your 'house', but acceptance from God of all that he has given you will bring joy and fulfilment.

a. Daughter

> '___________ your _____________ and your ___________ ,
> so that you may live long in the land the Lord your God
> is giving you.'
>
> (Exodus 20:12)

The Hebrew word for honour means 'to make weighty' or to 'give weight to'. Even though we are no longer children needing to obey our parents, we are not to disregard them, making light of their opinions and feelings. Rather, we are to *honour* them. If your parents are alive, are you expecting your relationship with them to grow? Are you 'giving weight to them'?

b. Sister

God moulds our character through family relationships. Make friends of your brothers and sisters. Reach out and bless them. If you don't have 'natural' brothers and sisters, be a real sister to your brothers and sisters in Christ who are close to you.

c. Mother/Grandmother/Aunt

Children are important to God:

> '*Little children were brought to Jesus for him to place his hands on them and pray for them. But the disciples rebuked those who brought them. Jesus said, "Let the*
>
> ___________ _______________ _________ _____ _____ ,
>
> *and do not hinder them, for the kingdom of heaven belongs to such as these."* '
>
> (Matthew 19:13-14)

Build relationships with the children in your life.

☐ Mother — build a warm, loving relationship with each of your children. Be diligent to train them (Proverbs 1:8).

☐ Grandmother — pray for your grandchildren; love them.

☐ Aunt — support the family. (Adopt one if necessary.)

Be interested in the well-being of each child.

d. Wife

Expect the relationship with your husband to be constantly growing, no matter how long you have been married.

> 'An excellent wife is the **crown** of her husband.'
>
> (Proverbs 12:4 NASB)

Are *you* your husband's joy and crown?

4. Building a Home

The joy and fulfilment of being a homemaker is God's plan for every woman, married or single. A stable, ordered home (whether an apartment for single girls, a room in lodgings or your own house) should be a place of security and blessing to yourself and of encouragement and blessing to all who come there.

Scripture records a number of occasions when Jesus stayed in the home of Lazarus and his two sisters, Mary and Martha (Luke 10:38-42; John 12:1-8). Jesus felt at home with these single people. Is your home a place where the Holy Spirit is free to motivate and direct as he chooses — where there isn't so much 'clutter', mentally and physically, that there is no room for him? Or is it a place where you are so house-proud and concerned about outward appearances that Jesus isn't at home there?

a. Some hindrances to building your home

1. *Society's attitude*

Society views a homemaker as being second-rate; only those without drive or intelligence stay at home and keep house. Single women, it is felt, should be career-minded and not concerned about homemaking.

2. *Mother's attitude*

Mother may have been house-proud to the extreme so that the family could not relax and enjoy the home. She may never have taken the trouble to train her daughters, leaving them to grow up with a feeling of inadequacy. Your childhood experience of home may have lacked warmth and happiness. You may consider home to be a place to get out of as soon as possible.

3. *Self-centredness*

'What about me? How will my needs be met if I give all my time and energy for others?' The basis for discontent in the home for many women is selfishness: 'I want to do my own thing — not to be a doormat for everyone else.'

4. *Feeling that it isn't spiritual enough*

'God has more important things for me to do than keep house!' If a woman hasn't learned to be content and at peace in her home, she will be restless and discontent in other areas of her life and ministry.

b. Bringing the home into order

> *'Encourage the young women . . . to be sensible, pure, workers at home . . . that the word of God may not be dishonoured.'*
> (Titus 2:4-5 NASB)

Everything God does he does decently and in order. If women fail to bring their homes into order, what does this verse say will be brought into disrepute?

'______ ________ ____ _______ .'

(Titus 2:5)

Our homes are to bring honour to Jesus. God wants to adjust any wrong attitudes and thinking and to teach us his way.

c. Being a good homemaker

This involves learning to find joy and fulfilment in each task we do for Jesus, creating an atmosphere of love and warmth, praise and thanksgiving in our homes.

It also involves:

- ☐ Inventiveness

- ☐ Organisation

- ☐ Efficiency

- ☐ Planning menus

- ☐ Creativity

- ☐ Order in cleaning

- ☐ Updating your methods

- ☐ Taking care of clothing

- ☐ Shopping and budgeting

These are all important to God. He wants you to *succeed* as a homemaker.

5. Conclusion

'To build' means to 'construct by successive additions'. God doesn't require us to do everything all at once, nor does he say, 'A wise woman *has* built her house,' but rather that she *is* building it. Allow the Holy Spirit to pin-point the prime areas in your life that you need to give attention to building at this time. Then diligently build, by successive additions, your relationships and home in a way that will glorify your Father.

* *

LESSON 2

The Wise Woman Builds Her House

True or False

1. T F If I diligently do all the tasks around my home and meet all the demands that are made on me, I will fulfil God's plan for me without needing to know his blueprint for my life.

2. T F Married women are more profitable to God than single women. Therefore, the sooner single girls get married the better.

3. T F As an adult, the role of mother is more important than the role of daughter. It therefore doesn't matter if we don't maintain a relationship with our parents.

4. T F Even if a woman is involved in evangelistic or other church activities, it is still important that her home is efficiently kept and managed.

5. T F Single girls have more opportunity to serve in the church; it isn't necessary for them to develop homemaking skills.

6. T F Some women are called to serve in the home, others are called to other things.

7. T F God desires every woman to be a good homemaker, even if she only has one room to make home.

8. T F Even in a very good marriage there is always more to come into.

9. T F We must desire to grow and develop our relationships or they will stagnate.

10. T F Grandmothers have an important role in influencing the spiritual lives of their grandchildren.

Group Discussion

1. If a woman gives herself to all that comes her way, and takes every day and week as it comes, why will she not necessarily fulfil what God has planned for her?

2. How can we overcome each of the four hindrances to building our homes listed in section 4(a) above? Can you think of any other hindrances?

Personal Assignment

1. a. In which of your God-given roles as daughter, sister, mother, grandmother, aunt or wife do you find the most joy and fulfilment? Give thanks to your heavenly Father for that. Write down two things you are going to do this week to further build that (these) relationship(s).

    b. In which of those roles do you feel you most need to improve? Consider the type of relationship you would like it to be in the future and list ways in which you are going to build towards having that relationship.

2. Consider prayerfully whether Jesus is at home in the place where you live:

    ☐ List the things you feel he enjoys in your home — happy atmosphere, cleanliness, etc. Be encouraged by these.

    ☐ List two things Jesus wants to adjust and bring his order to — for example, discipline in tackling jobs no-one else sees, such as letter writing.

True or False

1.F 2.F 3.F 4.T 5.F 6.F 7.T 8.T 9.T 10.T

The Wise and Prudent Woman

1. Introduction

'She speaks with wisdom.'

(Proverbs 31:26)

'Houses and wealth are inherited from parents, but a prudent wife is from the Lord.'

(Proverbs 19:14)

☐ What does it mean for a woman to be wise and prudent?

☐ Are these qualities inherent in some women and not in others?

☐ If your mother was a wise woman, does it follow that you will inherit her wisdom?

☐ Or are these qualities something that every woman — regardless of background, education and upbringing — can acquire?

God's plan and desire is to make every woman who bears his name wise and prudent. A prudent wife comes from the Lord (Proverbs 19:14). Wisdom and prudence are linked together:

*'I, _____________ , dwell together with _____________ ;
I possess knowledge and discretion.'*

(Proverbs 8:12)

What is wisdom and what is prudence?

Wise — Webster's Collegiate Dictionary defines wise as 'marked by deep understanding, keen discernment and a capacity for sound judgment'.

Prudent — This means 'wise in practical affairs, wisely cautious'. Another dictionary says, 'Having an eye for the future'.

The wisdom God gives has nothing to do with the natural and often conflicting advice offered by women's magazines, books and therapists: how to bring up children; how to deal effectively with the neighbours, the school, your boss at work and your in-laws; how to make the most of your garden or home; how to attract that good-looking man.

God has something to say about all of these and, indeed, every detail of our lives. Scripture gives the key to God's wisdom:

> *'The __________ of ______ __________ is the beginning of __________________ , and knowledge of the Holy One is understanding.'*

(Proverbs 9:10)

We will become wise women when we are more concerned about what *God* has to say than about what our mother-in-law or the doctor says, or what women in the world or the church will think of us. It is as we seek and search for God that we will have understanding. We will find out his way of handling our children, restoring broken relationships, living peacefully with the neighbours or deciding where to go on holiday.

Proverbs has this to say about a wise and prudent woman:

- ☐ She has a purposeful, ordered life.

- ☐ She has a teachable spirit.

- ☐ She is wise with her time.

- ☐ She is discreet and modest.

2. A Purposeful, Ordered Life

'The wisdom of the prudent is to give _______________
to [her] _________ . . . *a prudent [woman] gives thought*
to [her] _______ .'*

(Proverbs 14:8, 15)

In lesson 2 we saw that God has a blueprint for our lives. This passage again emphasises that the wise woman is not living a haphazard life but:

☐ She has sought God to know his plan and direction for her life.

☐ She is moving purposefully towards taking hold of all that for which God has taken hold of her (Philippians 3:12).

Have you asked God what he has planned for you in the next few years? What has he put in your heart to reach after and to be growing towards?

☐ To bring your home and family life into order?

☐ To serve his people in a particular gift area that he has given you?

Write down the things you are reaching for:

____

____

____

In the light of these goals, what needs to happen:

☐ In the next year?

☐ In the next six months?

☐ In the next month?

How does that affect the way you will live and plan your time this week? Are there attitudes and patterns of behaviour that you need to let God change in order for you to reach your goals?

3. A Teachable Spirit

a. Ready to learn

The book of Proverbs teaches us that wisdom comes with humility:

> *'When pride comes, then comes disgrace, but with ________________ comes ____________ .'*
>
> (Proverbs 11:2)

If we are to grow in wisdom and become prudent, our whole attitude must be one of reverence for the Lord and an openness to learn and be taught:

> *'________________ to ________________ and ____________ ________________ , and in the end you will be wise.'*
>
> (Proverbs 19:20)

> *'Listen to my ________________ and ____________ ;
> do not ignore it.'*
>
> (Proverbs 8:33)

The Holy Spirit will speak directly into your heart — through the Bible, through your husband or leaders, or through other brothers and sisters in Christ. When you are instructed in new methods of home management, or counselled in your marriage or in a strained relationship with a brother or sister, do you say, 'Yes, yes,' but then let it go after a few days when the going gets tough?

Proverbs 8:33 instructs, 'Do not ignore it.' How we receive such correction is a reflection of how much we fear the Lord and how much we *really* want to grow in wisdom.

> *'Whoever loves ______________________ loves*
> *____________ , but he who hates correction is stupid.'*
>
> (Proverbs 12:1)

> *'Do you see a [woman] ________ in [her] ______*
> *________ ? There is more hope for a ________ than for*
> *[her].'*
>
> (Proverbs 26:12)

The Bible says we are stupid if we don't love to be disciplined and reproved! If we won't receive counsel and correction, but insist on doing things our own way, there is no hope for our growing in God. Even the woman who claims, 'God has told me . . .', and is not open to hearing correction through her brothers and sisters in Christ, is a fool, the Bible says.

> *'A______________ ______________________ a [woman] of*
> *______________________ more than a hundred lashes*
> *a fool.'*
>
> (Proverbs 17:10)

☐ A woman who doesn't want to change can be taught, admonished and corrected again and again with no effect. Satan will find plenty of scope to bind, depress and hinder.

☐ But a woman who understands that the Lord corrects those he loves, disciplining them for their own good (Hebrews 12:5-6), will receive correction the first time — and the devil will have to flee.

b. Help from others

A woman with a teachable spirit will seek out others who will strengthen and encourage her to walk with God:

> *'[She] who ________ ________ ______ ________*
> *grows wise, but a companion of fools suffers harm.'*
>
> (Proverbs 13:20)

'[She] who listens to a __________-______________ __________ will be at home among the wise.'

(Proverbs 15:31)

'A mocker resents correction; [she] will not consult the wise.'

(Proverbs 15:12)

The woman who desires to grow in Christ will seek out those who will sharpen her. She will not avoid those whom she knows will give her the word of the Lord, nor those who will tell her the truth. She wants to hear, even though it may hurt. Women who live on the fringe, spending a lot of time chatting with those who don't fear the Lord, won't grow in wisdom but will fall into all kinds of mishap and evil (Proverbs 9:13-18).

4. Wise with Her Time

'Be careful how you walk, not as unwise [women] but as wise, making the most of your time, because the days are evil. So then do not be foolish, but understand what the will of the Lord is.'

(Ephesians 5:15-17 NASB)

a. Building her house

When you are clear about what God has given you to do at any particular stage in your life, then you *know* what the will of the Lord is. You are building your house. The challenge is now: Are you making the *most* of your time? Proverbs tells us to go to the ant, consider its ways and be wise:

'It has no commander, no overseer or ruler, yet it stores its provisions in summer and gathers its food at harvest.'

(Proverbs 6:7-8)

A wise woman isn't lazy, putting off until tomorrow what should be done today. Without being constantly reminded, she gets on with what she knows God has given her to do — in her home, her family and her job.

b. Using her free time

'Free time? What free time? I don't *have* any free time!' many women will exclaim. But if we are diligently building and working hard, it is important that we know how to rest and relax. The more limited the time, the more important it is to use it wisely.

> *'Whatever is true, whatever is noble, whatever is right, whatever is pure, whatever is lovely, whatever is admirable — if anything is excellent or praiseworthy — think about such things.'*
>
> (Philippians 4:8)

Are the things you read, watch or listen to adding to your growth in God, or are they detracting from it? You can't expect to be a better wife if the things you read in magazines and watch on television undermine the very principles God has established for marriage. Nor will you successfully fulfil your calling as a single woman if you continually feed your mind on romantic stories. If you are a wise woman you will make sure that the friendships you make, your hobbies and your interests will have a positive, upbuilding influence rather than a negative or undermining effect on you.

Your body is a temple of the Holy Spirit (1 Corinthians 6:19). Are you taking care of it with proper rest, food and exercise? God is more than willing to help any one of his daughters to bring her physical needs into line. He will guide you as to the type of foods that are good for you, the proper amounts and the right times to eat. He is very practical, if you ask him.

5. Discreet and Modest

Webster's Dictionary defines discretion as 'freedom of judgment or choice'. The Oxford Dictionary says, 'the liberty of suiting one's action to circumstances'. Modesty means, 'not excessive; pure-minded'. Proverbs says:

'Like a gold ring in a pig's snout is a beautiful woman who shows _____ ____________________ .'

(Proverbs 11:22)

A gold ring is both valuable and beautiful, but totally useless and out of place in a pig's nose! Valuable and beautiful are God's daughters to him, but if they haven't learned to suit their actions appropriately to the circumstances they meet, they will be ineffective for God in those circumstances:

'The woman of folly is boisterous, she is naive, and knows nothing. And she sits at the doorway of her house . . . calling to those who pass by, who are making their paths straight: "Whoever is naive, let him turn in here." '

(Proverbs 9:13-16 NASB)

This foolish woman not only puts herself in a place where she is exposed to temptation, but she also tempts others to stray from 'straight' paths and do evil. Women who allow themselves to get into situations where they are vulnerable will not only have to face the consequences themselves, but will also be accountable for distracting others from walking right with God:

'A wise [woman] is cautious and turns away from evil, but a fool is arrogant and careless.'

(Proverbs 14:16 NASB)

'A ____________ [woman] _________ _____________ and ____________ _______________ , but the simple keep going and suffer for it.'

(Proverbs 22:3)

Wise women are aware of the strong temptations and pressures on men. With the divorce rate rising to one in two marriages, it is evident that lust plays a large part in marriage break-up. A woman who is wise and prudent and who fears the Lord will go out of her way to make sure that she is *not* causing her brothers, married or single, to stumble. She will be careful how she dresses, making sure that what she wears is fit for the occasion, not excessive or calling attention to herself. She will consider her manner and behaviour that she in no way flaunts herself, but that these are appropriate for a daughter of the King of kings.

* *

LESSON 3

The Wise and Prudent Woman

True or False

1. T F To become a wise woman it is important to have a good education.

2. T F A prudent woman is cautious and 'tight' with money.

3. T F Some women are born prudent.

4. T F A prudent woman knows God's plan and direction for her life.

5. T F A woman is stupid if she doesn't love to be corrected.

6. T F If I believe God has spoken to me about something, I am wise to carry through with it, regardless of what others say.

7. T F A mark of wisdom in a woman is to know what she is about and not need others to stand with her.

8. T F A wise woman will make sure she has some free time.

9. T F As a woman, I am accountable if I allow myself to get into any vulnerable situations.

10. T F Women need not be concerned if their manner and behaviour is tempting to men — that's the men's problem.

Group Discussion

1. When a child gets sick, is it 'wise' to take him to the doctor straightaway?

2. Discuss situations where the world has certain expectations of us that are generally considered to be wise but are not necessarily wise in God's eyes.

3. If we have a close walk with God ourselves, why do we need to have fellowship with other women who are walking closely with the Lord?

4. Consider situations where women need to be especially careful about being discreet and modest.

5. In what ways can free time be spent that will refresh the body, edify the mind, build helpful relationships or help generally to relax?

Personal Assignment

1. Consider any situations recently where you acted rashly without considering the consequences, for example, you spoke too soon or unadvisedly, or you took on more than you could manage. What specifically can you learn from that and so grow in wisdom?

2. What was the last correction or reproof you received from the Lord? Did you welcome it? What are you doing about it?

3. List three people whom you know stir and sharpen you in your faith and walk with God. Do you actively seek fellowship with them? If not, why not?

4. Consider the last six months. Have there been times when your dress and/or your behaviour has been wrongly provocative to men? What changes are you going to make to become wise and so walk in the fear of the Lord?

True or False

1.F 2.F 3.F 4.T 5.T 6.F 7.F 8.T 9.T 10.F

Kindness is on Her Tongue

'She opens her mouth in wisdom, and the teaching of kindness is on her tongue.'

(Proverbs 31:26 NASB)

1. What *is* Kindness?

Webster's Dictionary defines *kind* as 'showing or having a gentle, considerate nature. Affectionate, loving, disposed to be helpful'.

Kindness is:

☐ Making other people feel at ease in unfamiliar situations.

☐ Sometimes letting a child do things himself and, where appropriate, letting him learn from his own mistakes.

☐ Not shouting at the children for leaving the bathroom in a mess, but training them how to tidy up after themselves.

☐ Going the second mile in helping your friend out when she has taken on too much.

☐ Understanding when your husband is tired and needs to relax and you have a list of urgent things for him to do.

☐ And thousands and thousands more!

'A gracious woman attains honour.'

(Proverbs 11:16 NASB)

Graciousness is closely allied to kindness and is defined by such words as 'pleasing, acceptable, courteous, generous of spirit'.

'Be _________ and ____________________ to one another, ________________ each other.'

(Ephesians 4:32)

'Love is _______________ , love is _________ .'

(1 Corinthians 13:4)

Most women have every intention of being kind and gracious to others. The majority sincerely desire to be compassionate and forgiving, but in the heat of the moment, the busyness of life, the unexpected developments of the day that cause tension and pressures to mount, their reactions explode in the unkind word, the unkind action (or even the unkind silence) or the thoughtless remark.

2. God is the Source of Kindness

Kindness and graciousness are part of God's character. Kindness is part of the fruit of the Holy Spirit listed in Galatians 5:22-23. It is only as we appreciate God's kindness to us that we can begin to express that kindness through our lives to others.

'The Lord is ________________ and compassionate.'

(Psalm 111:4)

'When the ________________ and _________ of God our Saviour appeared, he saved us.'

(Titus 3:4-5)

'[God] is __________ to the ungrateful and wicked.'

(Luke 6:35)

God is kind and his heart is full of lovingkindness towards his children. A study of Jesus' attitude to women in the gospels will reveal God's heart towards women in particular. Jesus never nagged at women, never flattered or patronised them. He gave both rebuke and praise as needed. He took their questions and arguments seriously. He had no axe to grind, no uneasy male pride to defend; he simply took women as he found them, never treating them as inferior in any way. He never belittled or degraded them. Women in the gospels were drawn to him because he understood them perfectly, loved them individually and demonstrated his love for them by giving his life for their sins.

Do you know Jesus like that? Do you know that he understands you perfectly and loves you individually? He knows when you are tense, uptight and under pressure. He knows when you feel left out or a nobody. He feels it when you feel uncared for and unnoticed. He loves you just the same when all your plans and good intentions have gone wrong and you know you have made a mess of things. You started the day right, but by eight o'clock it's all gone wrong.

> ' "Though the _________________ be _____________ and the hills be removed, yet my _____________________________ _________ for you will _______ be _______________ nor my covenant of peace be removed," says the Lord, who has compassion on you. "O afflicted city [woman], lashed by storms and not comforted, I will ___________ you with stones of turquoise, your foundations with sapphires. I will make your battlements of rubies, your gates of sparkling jewels, and all your walls of precious stones." '
>
> (Isaiah 54:10-12)

Though all around you may shake, though you be afflicted, storm-tossed and not comforted, God's kindness is *for* you.

But he doesn't want you to stay shaky and insecure. His promise to you is that, out of your helplessness and inability to change yourself, he will give you secure foundations and build the walls of your life strongly and securely — if you will let him. You will then no longer be storm-tossed and afflicted.

Start each day meditating on his kindness and love for you personally.

3. Kindness and the Tongue

'Out of the _________________ of the __________ the mouth __________ . The good man brings _________ things out of the good _____________ ____ in him, and the evil man brings evil things out of the evil stored up in him.'

(Matthew 12:34-35)

a. Evil hearts speak unkind words

Unforgiveness, fear and self-interest are evil:

- ☐ Unforgiveness towards a parent or child, husband, brother or sister in the church, your pastor or even civil authorities.

- ☐ Fear of what others think of you, fear of the future, fear of illness or death, fear of not getting married or fear that 'something may happen to the children'.

- ☐ Self-interest — my life, my home, my affairs, my job, my children, my ministry, my fulfilment and satisfaction, *me* first.

Allowed to stay in the heart, these things will defile you, making you insecure. It is from these things that hurtful, unkind words will come. They are not words of faith, but words of fear and self. Jesus said:

'What goes into a man's [or woman's] mouth does not make him "unclean", but what comes out of his __________ , that is what makes him "unclean" .... The things that come out of the mouth come from the __________ , and these make a man "unclean".'

(Matthew 15:11, 18)

Words are a powerful weapon for good or evil. What is in your heart will determine the kind of words that come out of your mouth and the effect they have, kind or unkind.

b. What to do with what's in your heart

> *'The _____________ is a _____________ part of the body, but it makes ___________ _____________ . Consider what a great forest is set on fire by a small spark.'*
>
> (James 3:5)

Generally speaking, women have a reputation for being talkers. Whether the reputation is justified or not, women (and men, for that matter) need to be able to 'talk out' their feelings. Women are generally sensitive and emotionally vulnerable and it is important that they are able to share their feelings and insights — for these are often God-given. Sadly, some husbands and churches don't make room for their wives or women to share their God-given wisdom and insights. But for most women the problem is not that of lacking freedom to share, but rather that of discerning between the God-given insights and the knotted up, frustrated ones!

1. In the family

☐ Husband

Perhaps your husband is not being the kind of husband you would like him to be — or, indeed, even the kind the Bible teaches he should be. You feel trapped. You must 'stay in submission'. Eventually your frustration erupts in a frontal attack of words — unkind words. Or perhaps you become more and more silent and kind words cease altogether.

But the truth is that *you are not trapped*. Go to your heavenly Father and pour out all the frustration. Submit yourself to him. Let him fill your heart with his love. Let him change you, and he will change your husband. Then share your feelings with your husband in a gentle spirit, with your trust in God. Remember: It is not so much *what* you say as *how* you say it that reveals your heart.

☐ Children

> *'Be kind and compassionate to one another, forgiving each other, just as in Christ God forgave you. Be imitators of God, therefore, as dearly loved children and live a life of love, just as Christ loved us and gave himself up for us.'*
>
> (Ephesians 4:32 — 5:2)

At times a mother's heart is overflowing with love for her children. It is easy then to forgive their misdemeanours. But at another time (a minute later!) she feels like banging their heads together! God's love isn't based on feelings, but on a *decision* to love:

> *'Live a life of love, just as Christ loved us.'*
>
> (Ephesians 5:2)

Decide before God that you will love your children, bringing each one up for him. Then speak kindly to them, disciplining and training them for God. Be in control.

2. In your friendships

> *'Do not let any unwholesome talk come out of your mouths, but only what is _______________________ for _______________ others up according to their needs, that it may _______________ those who listen.'*
>
> (Ephesians 4:29)

Are your friends encouraged and built up when you are around? Do the people you know look forward to seeing you, or are the things you talk about just empty chatter? Kindness is having a 'considerate nature'. A woman who desires to be kind will seek to consider the blessing of others in all she talks about. Even sharing your needs and difficulties can be done in a way that is uplifting to others, if your motive is one of consideration for them.

3. In the church

Women who don't live in the security of God's love and personal kindness towards them are potentially a very destructive element in the body of Christ. Out of their insecurity they will speak negative, undermining things, sowing their own doubts and fears into others.

Generally speaking, women have more opportunities than men to see one another during the day, more opportunity to talk things over. When you are together with other women, remember these simple rules:

i.   Only say about another person what you would be prepared to say if that person were present, and *only say it in the way you would say it if he or she were present.*

ii.   Never talk about people or situations that will in any way undermine them in others' eyes. Talk only of things that you can discuss positively and encouragingly.

iii. If you should hear someone talking negatively, don't just let it pass but bring the positive.

iv.   If there are things about which you have questions, things you are troubled or concerned about, don't bottle them up with excuses like, 'It's not my place to say anything.' Jesus is concerned that your mind is at rest and peace. Go to your husband and share your heart. Or go to your leaders; they are there to lead you, and God has given them to you for that purpose, so that you will be secure.

> *'Obey your leaders and submit to their authority. They ___________ ______________ over you as men who must _________ _______ ________________ . Obey them so that their work will be a joy, not a burden, for that would be of no advantage to you.'*
>
> (Hebrews 13:17)

c. Good hearts speak kind words

If your heart is full of God's goodness and kindness towards you, if you love him and are enjoying his love for you, these are the things that will come out of your mouth. Your tongue will *have* to speak about them:

- ☐ 'I felt so tired when I woke up this morning, but I know Jesus loves me. I know he will give me strength for today *and* show me how I can get some early nights!'

- ☐ 'The woman I work with is for ever complaining and consequently nothing seems to go right for her. I'd be like her if it wasn't for Jesus. Today, by God's grace, I'm going to treat her the way Jesus treats me.'

> *'A wise man's heart _______________ his mouth, and his lips _______________ instruction.'*
>
> (Proverbs 16:23)

Guide and teach your mouth to speak positive, good things that come from a heart of praise and thanksgiving for God's kindness. Enjoy his kindness to you, and it is easy to be kind to others:

> *'Let your conversation be always _________ ____ _________ [and kindness], seasoned with salt, so that you may know how to answer everyone.'*
>
> (Colossians 4:6)

Approach people with gentleness and speak kindly. In that attitude and frame of mind you will know how to respond to each person, adult or child.

- ☐ A squabble to sort out?

- ☐ An angry boss?

- ☐ An irate sales assistant?

☐ A domineering relative?

> *'The tongue of the _________ brings _________________ .'*
>
> (Proverbs 12:18)

> *'A gentle [or kind] answer turns away wrath, but a harsh word stirs up anger.'*
>
> (Proverbs 15:1)

4. Kind in Deed

a. Hospitality

The woman of Proverbs 31 not only had kindness on her tongue; she was known for her kind deeds:

> *'Her husband has full confidence in her . . . . She brings him good, not harm, all the days of her life.'*
>
> (Proverbs 31:11-12)

> *'She gets up while it is still dark; she provides food for her family and portions for her servant girls.'*
>
> (Proverbs 31:15)

> *'She opens her arms to the poor and extends her hands to the needy.'*
>
> (Proverbs 31:20)

The impression given concerning this woman is that her home was a thriving centre for all she was involved in. Whether it was going out to buy a field or planting a vineyard, she was doing her family good and watching over 'the affairs of her household' (v27).

> *'Offer hospitality to one another without grumbling.'*
>
> (1 Peter 4:9)

Webster's gives one meaning of the word *hospitable* as 'offering a pleasant or sustaining environment'. Does your home offer a pleasant environment for all who come into it? Is there warmth and kindness there?

If you always feel you must be on your best behaviour, provide special food and have nothing out of place, visitors and entertaining will be a pressure and a strain. Be yourself. Let the Holy Spirit show you how to make each person feel at home. Be more concerned for the *person* than for the hospitality you are providing:

> *'When you give a luncheon or dinner, do not invite your friends, your brothers or relatives, or your rich neighbours; if you do, they may invite you back and so you will be repaid. But when you give a banquet, invite the poor, the crippled, the lame, the blind, and you will be _____________ . . . they cannot repay you.'*
>
> (Luke 14:12-14)

b. Serving from the heart

There are endless opportunities on every hand to show kindness: the sick, the old and infirm, the lonely, the young mother who has just had a baby, the single-parent family, the bereaved. The needs can be quite overwhelming, but true kindness, as we have already seen, comes from a heart that has been touched by *God's* kindness. Out of love for Jesus, the Holy Spirit will direct each individual.

> *'Each one should use whatever gift he has received to _____________ _________ , faithfully administering God's grace in its various forms. If anyone speaks, he should do it as one speaking the very words of God. If anyone serves, he should do it with the strength God provides, so that in _________ _______________ _________ may be _________________ through Jesus Christ. To him be the glory and the power for ever and ever. Amen.'*
>
> (1 Peter 4:10-11)

5. Conclusion

Kindness comes from God. A woman who desires to grow in kindness must first be rooted securely in God's love and kindness herself. From that security she will know the freedom both to speak kindness and to do kind deeds for others. Without that constant reference-point of Jesus' love for her and his love through her for others, all her kind intentions will be a strain. She will live under the burden of 'I ought to'. But with Jesus as the source, her kindness will spring from liberty and joy in blessing others.

* *

LESSON 4

Kindness is on Her Tongue

True or False

1. T F Graciousness is a quality necessary only for the sophisticated and élite.

2. T F When our children are ungrateful, we shouldn't reward them with kindness.

3. T F God is only kind to those who respond to his kindness.

4. T F If we are not sure of God's love and kindness towards us, we will find it hard to be kind to others.

5. T F Because God's lovingkindness is towards us, it doesn't matter to him if we are 'afflicted' and 'storm-tossed'; he will just continue to comfort us.

6. T F God's kindness will result in what for a time may be painful foundation work in our lives.

7. T F Kindness is just saying nice things about other people to make them feel good.

8. T F Only words that are said sincerely, in truth and love, are really kind.

9. T F A truly submissive woman will be careful about sharing the negative things she is feeling in her heart lest she hurt those concerned.

10. T F Being kind to her children is a decision that a mother must make, based on obedience to God rather than a response to her emotions.

11. T F The attitude and frame of mind in which we approach people will affect the way we speak to them.

12. T F It is part of every woman's role to be hospitable.

13. T F A kind woman will try to meet every need she sees.

14. T F Our kindness, if initiated by the Holy Spirit, will bring glory to Jesus.

Group Discussion

1. How does the kindness shown by the world differ from the kindness that is part of the fruit of the Holy Spirit?

2. Share together experiences you have had when your own lack of security in God's love has produced an unkind reaction. Also share times when, naturally speaking, you would have reacted unkindly but because you knew God's love you were able to respond with kindness. Encourage and pray for one another.

Personal Assignment

1. Consider the situations where you find it most difficult to be genuinely kind, from the heart, for example, children's bedtime — the children are tired, you are tired and your husband isn't going to be home until late. Consider: Do you pass your pressure on to the children or do you know God as a kind Father who understands and can give you supernatural strength? Ask God to reveal his love to you in each situation and then draw on his kindness this week.

2. Are there certain people to whom you find it hard to be kind? Write their names down and then ask God to show you why you find it difficult in each case. Put right any wrong on your part, for example, jealousy, nursed hurts or unforgiveness. Then pray for each person and expect God to show you specific ways you can start expressing the kindness of God to them.

3. If you begrudge people coming into your home, ask God to give you a liberal spirit and to teach you ways of being welcoming. Go out of your way to invite those who can't repay you.

4. If you know that you are often insensitive to the needs of others, ask the Holy Spirit to prompt you and show you when they need help. Cultivate sensitivity to the Holy Spirit in this regard.

True or False

1.F 2.F 3.F 4.T 5.F 6.T 7.F 8.T 9.T 10.T 11.T 12.T 13.F 14.T

The Faithful Woman

1. Introduction

The book of Proverbs has much to say about the unfaithful woman. The writer warns us again and again not to get involved with her.

She is described as:

☐ A wayward and adulterous woman who flatters with her lips (2:16).

☐ A woman who forsakes her husband and the partner of her youth (2:17).

☐ A woman who ignores and breaks her covenant with God (2:17).

☐ A loose or adulterous woman whose talk is smooth and sweet but who in the end brings much bitterness and heartache (5:3-4).

☐ A woman who lives aimlessly, not considering the way of life (5:6).

If these are the descriptions of an unfaithful woman, what is a faithful woman? Webster's Dictionary defines *faithful* as:

☐ Full of faith.

☐ Steadfast in action or allegiance.

☐ True to an original.

2. Full of Faith

The faithful woman is full of faith:

> *'In the gospel a righteousness from God is revealed, a righteousness that is by faith from first to last, just as it is written: "The righteous [woman] will ________ ____ __________ ." '*

(Romans 1:17)

As a woman of God you have been called to live by faith in every area of your life — your health, your finances, your home and family, your job. Your whole life is to be lived by, and increasing in, faith. (For a full definition and study on faith see the School of the Word study *According to Your Faith,* by Bryn Jones, Harvestime, 1985.)

In order to grow in faith you must first have faith in the following areas:

a. Faith in God's forgiveness of the past

Women have a tendency to live in the land of 'if only': 'If only I didn't come from a broken home.' 'If only I'd become a Christian when I was younger.' 'If only I hadn't got involved with that man.' 'If only I hadn't done this or that.'

You will never be a woman of faith if you don't put your faith in God's forgiveness of the past. If you have confessed your sin and asked forgiveness from God and those concerned, your failure and sin are gone:

> *' "They will all know me, from the least of them to the greatest," declares the Lord. "For I will ________________ their wickedness and will ________________ their sins ____ ________ ." '*

(Jeremiah 31:34)

God doesn't just forget our sin, or else he might remember it again at any time. Rather, he *chooses* not to remember it any more.

Sarai, the wife of Abram, who became the great man of faith Abraham, failed God and her husband many times. God had promised Abram a son and, though an old man, he believed God. But Sarai was impatient with God's timing and took things into her own hands:

> *'She said to Abram, "The Lord has kept me from having children. Go, sleep with my maidservant; perhaps I can build a family through her." Abram agreed to what Sarai said.'*
>
> (Genesis 16:2)

Women who aren't walking in faith themselves exert a strong, undermining pressure on a man's faith. Are you putting pressure on men because of a lack of faith yourself? When things didn't turn out the way she expected, Sarai blamed Abram:

> *'You are responsible for the wrong I am suffering. I put my servant in your arms, and now that she knows she is pregnant, she despises me.'*
>
> (Genesis 16:5)

Later, God sent angelic messengers to Abram, confirming that a son would be born to Sarai. Sarai (now renamed Sarah) overheard the conversation and secretly laughed to herself. Not only did she mock the man God sent but, when questioned about it, she lied to cover it up:

> *'Sarah was afraid, so she lied and said, "I did not laugh." '*
>
> (Genesis 18:15)

Have you ever secretly despised God's word to your husband or the leaders of your church? Be careful!

Even after her baby was born, Sarah was still sorting out her frustrations with the imperfect circumstances that were of her own making:

> *'Sarah saw that the son whom Hagar the Egyptian had borne to Abraham was mocking, and she said to Abraham, "Get rid of that slave woman and her son, for that slave woman's son will never share in the inheritance with my son Isaac." The matter distressed Abraham greatly because it concerned his son.'*
>
> (Genesis 21:9-11)

Are you depressed by your mistakes and the tangles you have got yourself into? Tell God about it and then let him work it out. Years later, Sarah must have been humbled and her heart must have melted before God as she saw how God's plan had been to bless her all along and to work out his purposes through her.

In the New Testament, God has this to say about Sarah:

> *'By faith even Sarah herself received ability to conceive, even beyond the proper time of life, since she considered him faithful who had promised.'*
>
> (Hebrews 11:11 NASB)

No mention of her lack of faith! In 1 Peter, God holds Sarah up as an example for us to follow:

> *'This is the way the holy women of the past who put their hope in God used to make themselves beautiful. They were _____________________ to their own husbands, ________ __________ , who obeyed Abraham and called him her master. ___________ are ____________ _________________ if you do what is right and do not give way to fear.'*
>
> (1 Peter 3:5-6)

God chose not to remember the times when she was not submissive to Abraham, when she did *not* believe God, when she took things into her own hands, manipulating people and circumstances to get her own way. Having forgiven, God chose only to remember and record the good things about Sarah. He chose only to remember the times when *she* did get it right.

God does the same for you. Put your faith in his choosing not to remember the times you have failed him. He chose you. Let your faith rise because of his faith in you.

b. Faith in God's choice of you

In lesson 1 we saw that, as a child of God, you have no right to reject yourself. You are bought by God — his own possession. But he didn't choose you just to look pretty and to make up the numbers in the church. He has faith in his own ability to make your life a trophy of his victory:

> 'Thanks be to God, who in Christ always leads us in triumph — as trophies of Christ's victory — and through us spreads and makes evident the fragrance of the knowledge of God everywhere.'
>
> (2 Corinthians 2:14 Amp)

In order to grow in faith, put your faith in his. He has faith for your finances, that you should have all you need and enough to give away. He has faith for you to be in complete health. He has faith for those areas of constant failure and weakness in you. He can make them strong. He has faith for your marriage — every part of it. He can make it better than you ever dreamed of. He has faith for you as a single to be a completely fulfilled woman — radiating Jesus' victory in your life. He has faith for you to be a fully functioning member of his church, bearing much fruit.

He chose you. Join your faith with his.

> *'Being ________________ of this, that he who began
> a good work in you will carry it on to ________________
> until the day of Christ Jesus.'*
>
> (Philippians 1:6)

3. Steadfast in Action and Allegiance

> *'________________ by itself, if it is not accompanied by
> ________________ , is dead. But someone will say, "You have
> faith; I have deeds." Show me your faith without deeds,
> and I will show you my faith by what I do.'*
>
> (James 2:17-18)

As a woman, full of faith, the whole way you live your life will show that faith. Your actions, your speech and your heart allegiance to Jesus will show you to be a faithful woman.

a. Faithful to husband

> *'Her husband has ________ ________________
> ____ ______ and lacks nothing of value. She brings him
> good, not harm, all the days of her life.'*
>
> (Proverbs 31:11-12)

The faithful woman earns her husband's confidence and trust. He can rely on her love, support and prayer. She always does him good, encouraging and helping him to become the man God wants him to be. She prayerfully cultivates an attitude of honour and esteem for him as her husband, running their home and caring for their children in a way that is pleasing to him. Are you doing your husband good? Can he fully trust you?

b. Faithful to brothers and sisters in God's family

*'Make my joy complete by being ________-_________ ,
having the same _________ , being _______ ______
_________ and ___________ . Do nothing out of
selfish ambition or vain conceit, but in humility
______________ _____________ better than
yourselves. Each of you should look not only to your own
interests, but also to the interests of others.'*

(Philippians 2:2-4)

As a faithful sister to your brothers and sisters in Christ, your heart attitude will be one of esteem, looking to bring out the best in them. Never think ill or in an undermining way of anyone. If your heart is not self-seeking or contentious you will neither bear grudges nor be jealous.

With a heart full of love and desire for others' blessing, a faithful woman will not be afraid to speak the truth to them for fear of wounding them. If you can see a fault in a brother or sister and you don't do anything about it, you aren't being a faithful sister. Pray for that person and ask God if there is anything he wants *you* to do.

*'A gossip betrays a confidence, but a trustworthy
[woman] _________ __ __________ .'*

(Proverbs 11:13)

'Faithful are the wounds of a friend.'

(Proverbs 27:6 NASB)

☐ A faithful woman doesn't gossip.

☐ A faithful woman looks for ways in word and action to encourage her brothers and sisters in one purpose — readiness for the return of the King of kings.

c. Faithful to leaders

> *'Miriam the prophetess, Aaron's sister, took a tambourine in her hand, and all the women followed her, with tambourines and dancing. Miriam sang to them: "Sing to the Lord, for he is highly exalted. The horse and its rider he has hurled into the sea." '*

(Exodus 15:20-21)

These women were responding to a song of triumph from the men after Moses had successfully led them across the Red Sea. Three days later:

> *'When they came to Marah, they could not drink its water because it was bitter . . . . So the people grumbled against Moses, saying, "What are we to drink?" '*

(Exodus 15:23-24)

These women could sing and dance when things were going well but they had no faith in God when their needs didn't appear to be getting met. God had shown Moses how to cross the Red Sea and where to get water. Instead of holding fast in faith, they grumbled and complained.

Are you faithful to the leaders in your church, even when things don't appear to be going the way you feel they should? Or do you begin to grumble and question the leadership's direction? A woman of faith puts her trust firmly in God and his ability to lead his church through his appointed leaders. They may not always get it right, but they are much more likely to do so with women who are faithful to them in prayerful encouragement and support.

4. **True to God's 'Original'**

a. Faithful to God's vision

When we look at the state of the world and the church across the world, there doesn't appear to be much hope for either. To be faithful women we have to look at the facts as *God* sees them. What was his original intention?

1. A glorious church

God is restoring his church to something more beautiful and glorious than this world has ever seen. Jesus is going to return to a church that is without spot or wrinkle — a church that has inherited all his promises. That was — and still is — God's original plan.

The Israelite women in Exodus had a similar vision. God had promised to deliver them from the slavery of Egypt and to give them health and wealth in a land 'flowing with milk and honey'. And they were all for it!

2. When the trials come

Yet those women had no faith. When God moved with signs and wonders, they sang his praises. But when trials came, they were the first to complain: 'No water, and the kids are crying with thirst!' 'No meat? We were better off in Egypt!' 'Manna? Not again!'

Can't you just see those women putting the pressure on the men to *do something*? The men in turn made their discontent known to Moses and Aaron. The women weren't faithful to the vision God had given them, but were tossed about by their circumstances and feelings — up one day and down the next.

3. Maintaining your faith

Are you faithful to what God has shown you? Or do you doubt his Word, his plan and his purposes as soon as obstacles and trials come? Are you a grumbler and complainer in the church, muttering your discontent or silently withdrawing your support? Perhaps you've moved house or even church in obedience to the Lord, but now the excitement has gone and you're tempted to doubt the rightness of the move. Be faithful to God and to his original word.

Your dream (and you felt sure it was from God) was to serve the Lord with your husband in some responsibility in the church. Perhaps even full time! But now you have a toddler and a baby, and your life is one round of nappies and feeds. When you *do* get to meetings, you don't feel you take in much, anyway. Everyone else is growing so much faster than you, it seems.

> *'Mary _________________ _____ all these things and _______________ them in her heart.'*
>
> (Luke 2:19)

Be faithful to God in all he is giving you to do now. Do the nappies/dishes/housework for God! But don't throw away your vision. In his time and in his way he will bring to pass what he has purposed.

b. Faith in his promises

Faith comes from a heart relationship with a loving God:

> *'The eyes of the Lord run to and fro throughout the whole earth, to show himself strong on behalf of those whose heart is loyal [perfect — King James Version] to him.'*
>
> (2 Chronicles 16:9 RAV)

To have a perfect heart doesn't mean you never make mistakes. It means you are devoted to God, loyal, dedicated and faithful to him. He then promises to show himself strong on your behalf.

LESSON 5

The Faithful Woman

True or False

1. T F A faithful woman follows behind her husband without saying anything.

2. T F A faithful woman meticulously follows the rules laid down by her church, regardless of what they are.

3. T F A faithful woman is on fire for God.

4. T F A faithful woman doesn't make mistakes.

5. T F God has more faith for some women than for others.

6. T F How we receive God's faithfulness to us will affect how much faith we have.

7. T F As women, just doing the things we have to do — housework, etc. — qualifies us as faithful women.

8. T F The way in which we live our lives towards God determines whether or not we are faithful.

9. T F Living by faith merely means that we have no regular source of income.

Group Discussion

1. If you are disturbed in your spirit about a particular change the leadership has brought in your church, what should you, as a faithful woman, do about it?

2. Share together experiences you have had of remaining faithful to God in your heart and attitude and seeing him work out 'impossible' situations for you.

Personal Assignment

1. Are you allowing past failure in your life to stop you growing in faith now? If so, deliberately tell God about it and put your faith in his forgiveness. This week, look for ways to step out on his faithfulness. Expect to grow in faith.

2. List two things that you can do to express your faithfulness to your husband (if you are married), to specific brothers and sisters in Christ and to the leaders of your church. Do them!

True or False

1.F 2.T 3.T 4.F 5.F 6.T 7.F 8.T 9.F

The Woman Who Fears the Lord

'A woman who fears the Lord is to be praised.'

(Proverbs 31:30)

The word *fear* in the Bible is used to translate several different Greek words with various meanings. For example, *phobos* is caused by being scared. It implies dread and terror, but it also means 'reverential fear'. Webster's New Collegiate Dictionary gives these definitions:

Fear =

☐ 'Profound reverence and awe, especially of God'.

Reverence =

☐ 'Honour or respect felt or shown'.

☐ 'Profound, adoring, awed respect'.

☐ 'The emotion inspired by what arouses one's deep respect'.

Revere =

☐ 'To show devoted, deferential honour to'.

☐ 'Stresses deference and tenderness of feeling'.

☐ 'Sincerity and simplicity'.

Synonyms for *revere* are 'venerate, worship, adore'.

How, in practice, does a woman fear the Lord?

1. Give Him Your Whole Self

*'Do not _______________ any other gods or bow down
to them, ___________ them or ___________________ to
them. But _______ ___________ , who brought you up out of
Egypt with mighty power and outstretched arm, is the
one you must worship. To him you shall bow down and
to him offer sacrifices.'*

(2 Kings 17:35-36)

The God who delivered us from the kingdom of darkness and
brought us into the kingdom of his own Son by the power of his
blood and his outstretched arms, the God who loves us with all his
heart, demands that devotion to him be the controlling motive of
our lives.

*'If anyone comes to me and does not _________ his
___________________ and _______________ , his _________
and _________________ , his _________________ and
_____________ — yes, even his ______ _________ — he
cannot be my disciple.'*

(Luke 14:26)

Nothing and no-one is to come between us and our love for Jesus.
The word *hate* here means 'by comparison with his love for me'.
The woman who fears the Lord has put Jesus on the unrivalled
throne of her heart. No-one in her life is more important than Jesus
himself.

2. Worship Him

In worshipping God you are acknowledging him for who he is and
for all he can do. He is your King and your Lord. He can control
all the circumstances of your life. Nothing is too difficult for him.
Worship implies that you are bowing before him in total surrender
and submission.

a. In truth

When Jesus talked with a Samaritan woman he shared with her the remarkable truth that the important thing isn't *where* we worship, or what style of worship we feel suits us best, but the *spirit* in which we worship:

> *'True worshippers will worship the Father in* ___________
> *and* __________ *, for they are the kind of worshippers*
> *the Father seeks.'*
>
> (John 4:23)

You can't truly worship God if you are chafing in your heart about a decision your husband has made, or the way the meeting is being led. You can sing songs and mouth words, but you can't worship God if you aren't in close fellowship with him, or if you are out of fellowship with a brother or sister. You can't worship God if in your heart you are holding on to worry and anxiety about the children or your job.

> *'You will fill me with joy in your presence.'*
>
> (Psalm 16:11)

Let go of your worry, fears and rebellious attitudes, and as you worship him you will know the joy of his presence.

b. With extravagance

Read Luke 7:37-47. This woman wasn't concerned what others would think of her as she 'wasted' expensive perfume on Jesus' feet, washing them with her tears and drying them with her hair.

As she worships, a woman who fears the Lord will be more concerned about Jesus himself than about what others are thinking of her. She won't be afraid to worship him with all that is within her. No act of worship is too extravagant in comparison with Jesus himself and what he has done for her.

3. Walk in His Ways

His way is a way of trust, meekness and thankfulness.

a. Freedom from fear

> 'This is the way the holy women of the past who put their hope in God used to make themselves beautiful. They were submissive to their own husbands, like Sarah, who obeyed Abraham and called him her master. You are her daughters if you do what is right and **do not give way to fear**.'
>
> (1 Peter 3:5-6)

Women generally are prone to fear — to be anxious and distracted by many things. Instead of being poised under pressure (one definition of meekness!), the temptation is to get uptight and panic when things don't go according to your plan. When the unexpected happens, or lots of little things pile up on you, you begin to expect the worst:

> '_______________ ________ __________ *and turn from wrath;* ____ ______ ________ *– it leads only to evil.*'
>
> (Psalm 37:8)

> '*The* ________ *will inherit the land and enjoy great* __________ .'
>
> (Psalm 37:11)

You may be tempted to lose your peace, get angry or adopt a 'disaster mentality'. But if you give way to these, you will not only feel confused and unable to hear God, but you will adversely affect those around you. Fretting always leads to wrong actions and reactions.

> '*You who fear him,* ___________ *in the Lord — he is their help and shield.*'
>
> (Psalm 115:11)

Trust in God and allow him to form in you:

b. A gentle and quiet spirit

> *'Your beauty should not come from outward adornment,
> such as braided hair and the wearing of gold jewellery
> and fine clothes. Instead, it should be that of your inner
> self, the _________________ _____________ of a
> ____________ and _____________________ , which is of
> great worth in God's sight.'*
>
> (1 Peter 3:3-4)

Of great worth, perhaps, because of its *rarity*. This attribute doesn't
come naturally to any man or woman (Galatians 5:22-23). It is a
characteristic of Jesus himself, who said:

> *'Take my yoke upon you and learn from me, for I am
> gentle and humble in heart, and you will find rest for your
> souls. For my yoke is easy and my burden is light.'*
>
> (Matthew 11:29-30)

When you stop trying to persuade God to do things your way, to
control your husband or circumstances — when, deep down inside,
you let him take control — then you know his gentleness. You enjoy
his inner stillness and rest in the middle of trouble and upsets. Your
confidence is in God.

For this meek and gentle spirit to be formed in us we must respond
to the promptings of the Holy Spirit and allow him to control our
reactions. If new patterns of thought and behaviour are to be
established in us, we must respond to him time after time, crisis
after crisis. A woman who fears the Lord will cultivate this
dependence upon him until fretting is no longer a habit, but is
exchanged for rest and peace.

c. A thankful heart

'Give _________ in ______ ___________________ ,
for this is God's will for you in Christ Jesus.'

(1 Thessalonians 5:18)

Being thankful is God's will for you, part of walking in his ways. The woman who fears the Lord will look for the positive in every situation she faces. If you believe God has your best interests at heart, you can be grateful to him no matter how bad things appear. You are no longer trying to control your own affairs or persuade God to do things your way. You have 'let go' to God, and deep down you have peace. Thanksgiving and praise are the natural outflow of peaceful, joyful lives:

'You who fear the Lord, _____________ _______ !'

(Psalm 22:23)

4. Serve and Obey Him

'If you fear the Lord and _________ and ________ him
and do not rebel against his commands, and if . . . you
follow the Lord your God — good!'

(1 Samuel 12:14)

A woman who fears the Lord is convinced of her individual calling. She knows she isn't lost in the crowd because it is vital to God's purposes that she fulfil all that God has called her to.

'[She] whose walk is upright fears the Lord, but [she]
whose ways are devious despises him.'

(Proverbs 14:2)

The woman who knows what she should be doing, and gets on and does it, fears the Lord. Even the doing of so-called 'little' tasks, when done in sincerity and simplicity, is a way of reverencing the Lord.

But putting off the cleaning or the mending with excuses (to cover up laziness) is to despise him.

We aren't called to 'do as we are told' but to have a spirit that delights to do his will:

> *'Mary . . . sat at the Lord's feet listening to what he said.'*
>
> (Luke 10:39)

As we listen to Jesus each day we will hear his individual instructions to us.

> *'Whoever wants to be first must be your slave — just as the Son of Man did not come to be served, but to* ___________ *, and to give his life as a ransom for many.'*
>
> (Matthew 20:27-28)

For most women, much of their daily life is spent in serving others — husbands, children, teenagers, bosses, friends and neighbours. Jesus knew what it was to serve in domestic affairs — resolving a drinks shortage at a wedding, washing disciples' feet, feeding hungry people. When his discouraged followers returned from a fruitless night's fishing, he had a cheerful fire burning, breakfast cooking and a call to 'come and eat'. (The risen Lord of glory had built the dirty fire and gutted the smelly fish.)

The woman who fears the Lord delights to serve this Jesus in every way she can.

5. Love Him

The words *reverence* and *revere* carry in their definition the sense of 'profound adoring' and 'tenderness of feeling'.

The woman who fears the Lord, honouring and respecting him, can't help but find her heart filled with love for the one who loves her so much and who proves himself so worthy of her devotion. As she allows that love to well up inside her, there are countless ways in which she can express that love for him. Not always in big, dramatic ways, but sometimes quiet heart-response to him that no-one else knows about:

☐ Rising early, simply to be alone with him.

☐ Going the extra mile in serving that difficult person, just for his sake.

☐ Doing more than is required, in secret, just to bring joy to his heart:

> *'On the first day of the week, very early in the morning, the women took the spices they had prepared and went to the tomb.'*
> (Luke 24:1)

These were women whose lives had been touched and transformed by Jesus' love and concern for them. Now they hurried to anoint his cold, stiff body with spices — long before the disciples were on the scene. Such was their love. But we have a glorious, loving, *living* Lord Jesus. Do you show him how much *you* love him?

Parts of his body here on earth are cold and stiff. Do you avoid such people, despising them in your heart? Or do you reach out to them in love, for his sake, caring and warming, and setting them free where they are imprisoned?

The woman who fears the Lord loves him and his people with all her heart.

6. Conclusion

> *'The Lord commanded us . . . to fear the Lord our God, so that we might always prosper and be kept alive.'*
> (Deuteronomy 6:24)

God promises many blessings to those who fear the Lord: health, prosperity, long life, to name just a few. God wants to give us *abundant* life.

> *'What does the Lord your God ask of you but to fear the Lord your God, to ________ ____ ______ ______ ________ , to love him, to ____________ the Lord your God ________ ______ _________ _______________ and with all your soul, and to ____________________ _________ ________ _______________ and decrees that I am giving you today for your own good?'*
>
> (Deuteronomy 10:12-13)

* *

LESSON 6

The Woman Who Fears the Lord

True or False

1. T F A woman who knows the fear of the Lord is terrified of displeasing him.

2. T F Reverence is an emotion provoked by someone we respect.

3. T F To fear the Lord involves sacrifice.

4. T F If you are anxious and worried, you can't truly worship God.

5. T F When we worship God with others we should be careful not to offend them in the way we worship.

6. T F When we procrastinate we are not walking in the fear of the Lord.

7. T F Some women naturally have a meek and gentle spirit.

8. T F The quiet spirit that God so prizes in a woman is formed by the ongoing work of the Holy Spirit in her life.

9. T F Anxious thinking leads to sin.

10. T F Thankfulness comes from a submissive heart.

11. T F A woman who wants to serve God must have a recognised ministry in the church.

12. T F It is possible to love God without loving his people.

Group Discussion

1. Explain what it means to 'hate' father, mother, children, etc., in order to be a disciple of Jesus. How does this relate to fearing the Lord with an undivided heart?

2. Share together examples of times when you have experienced the blessings of fearing the Lord rather than man (or other women).

3. Give examples of situations where a 'meek and gentle spirit' is most hindered. In those situations what is the root of the hindrance? Example: You are annoyed because your husband forgot to tell you he had an evening engagement and you had expected him to fix things around the house that evening. Root cause: My plans, my will, were upset.

Personal Assignment

1. Using a concordance, make a list of the benefits God promises to those who fear him.

2. Prayerfully go through the five ways of fearing the Lord listed in this lesson. For each one, write down how you personally are living in the fear of the Lord. Also write down changes that you need to make in this regard and talk specifically about them with the Lord.

True or False

1.F 2.T 3.T 4.T 5.F 6.T 7.F 8.T 9.T 10.T 11.F 12.F

A Woman of Strength

1. Introduction

☐ 'I can do it myself, thank you.'

☐ 'No, I can manage perfectly well on my own.'

☐ 'I've never had help before and I'm certainly not going to accept it now.'

Women who can boast that they have never needed help, who compete with other women or even men to prove their own ability and independence, are often admired for their strength. But this isn't the strength God commends in a woman.

No-one wants to feel dependent on others or obligated to someone else. Yet the strong-willed determination to 'make it on my own', to 'make my point', or 'defend my rights' produces a hardness and independence that doesn't reflect the meekness and gentleness of Christ. Even a Christian woman who seemingly does all the right things — keeping her home in order and being very active in the church — can have an independent attitude, making it hard for others to relate to her. She can't receive from them and so deprives them of the joy of giving. This is her weakness, not her strength.

Not so the woman of Proverbs 31:

> *'She girds herself with strength, and makes her arms strong.'*
>
> (Proverbs 31:17 NASB)

'Spiritual, mental and physical fitness for her God-given task' is how the Amplified Bible enlarges on this verse. What does it mean to be 'strong in God'? How does a Christian woman 'clothe herself with strength'?

Definitions:

Strong =

☐ 'Not easily disturbed, or torn or worn or injured or captured'.

☐ 'Tough, firm, healthy' (Oxford English Dictionary).

☐ 'Having great resources' (Webster's New Collegiate Dictionary).

2. Not Easily Disturbed

'She is clothed with _______________ and ___________ .'
(Proverbs 31:25)

In lesson 1 we saw that knowing who you are — a daughter of the King, accepted and chosen by him — brings security. You don't have to *prove* your worth. He has *made* you worthy. Coming to rest in this fact makes you strong:

> *'Thus said the Lord God, the Holy One of Israel, "In returning to me and resting in me you shall be saved; in quietness and in (trusting) confidence shall be your strength." '*

(Isaiah 30:15 Amp)

A woman who relies on her own abilities and self-effort is easily disturbed. She doesn't have inner peace, but frustration or a martyr attitude: 'Poor me. No-one knows what I carry. No-one appreciates all the hard work I do. I'm just taken for granted.' But in coming to Jesus and allowing him to work through her, in confidently trusting him for every detail of life, there is *strength*. When we are quietly trusting him and know a godly dependence on those whom he has given us (husband, brothers and sisters in Christ), we are not easily disturbed.

3. Not Easily Broken or Torn

'The way of the Lord is strength and a stronghold to the upright.'

(Proverbs 10:29 Amp)

Obedience to the way God has shown you to live as a woman, through his Word, is the secret of knowing his strength. Failure to live within the confines of God's Word is a major cause of 'broken' women, who are torn by conflicting demands, discontent, turmoil, strife and tension. But a woman who is 'building her house' with a lifestyle and relationships that are pleasing to God will grow from strength to strength. A woman who knows her God-given priorities at any time, diligently giving herself to those priorities, will know an inner peace and rest.

For the married woman, broadly speaking, this means:

☐ Her relationship with God.

☐ Loving and pleasing her husband; meeting his needs.

☐ Caring for the emotional, practical and spiritual needs of her children, including keeping her home in an orderly manner.

And then, with what time is left:

☐ Serving others in the church and community at large.

☐ Her job.

For the single woman it involves:

☐ Her relationship with God.

☐ Her relationship with her brothers and sisters in Christ with whom God has joined her — maintaining her love and commitment to them and from them.

☐   Her job.

☐   Her service to others in the church and community at large.

A woman who knows God's way for her and is obedient to him in it is clothing herself with strength.

4. Not Easily Worn or Injured

'I just feel so worn out, I can't go on.'

'Things aren't working out in my life the way I felt they should.'

'I had such faith that God was leading us and now we seem to have nothing but hardship and setbacks. Everything seems to be going wrong.'

> *'Do not grieve, for the _______ of the Lord is your _____________ .'*

(Nehemiah 8:10)

How can you know joy when the circumstances of your life seem grievous?

> *'You fill me with _______ in _________ _______________ .'*

(Psalm 16:11)

When you are walking in fellowship with God as a daughter with her Father — when you know there is no cloud of unconfessed sin, and your trust is in him — then you can experience the joy of his presence. Joy is the fruit of his Spirit working in your life. Joy is a bubbling up from deep within you that isn't dependent on circumstances.

Some women are happy with their circumstances but don't know lasting joy. When things go wrong they are easily hurt and worn out. When such a woman's boss at work is in a good mood and approves of her work, she is happy, but when he is under pressure and takes it out on her, she is injured. Maybe it is her children or husband who rob her of her happiness. But the joy of the Lord enables a woman to live above her circumstances, with a song in her heart, a twinkle in her eye and a strength that comes from God:

> *'Consider it pure _____________ , my [sisters], whenever you face trials of many kinds, because you know that the _____________ of your faith develops _____________ .'*
>
> (James 1:2-3)

5. Not Easily Captured

> *'Adam was not the one deceived; it was the _____________ who was _____________ and became a sinner.'*
>
> (1 Timothy 2:14)

Women, generally speaking, are prone to being deceived. It may be by the advertisement on TV, or the sales assistant who convinces her that the latest gadget is an absolute necessity that will transform her life. Or it may be by some new teaching that promises her a successful Christian life without trail or tribulation. She is 'captured' by many things.

> *'With him are wisdom and strength, he has counsel and understanding.'*
>
> (Job 12:13 RAV)

For a woman to become strong and not easily captured and led astray, she must depend on the Lord's wisdom, not her own. She must acknowledge her own vulnerability and actively seek to develop her dependence on God for wisdom and strength to withstand temptation.

Her dependence on God for wisdom on major issues will be expressed through her seeking counsel from those whom God has given her — her husband, church leaders, and other brothers and sisters in Christ whom she recognises as being wiser and more mature in Christ than herself. A woman who knows what it is to depend on God and others whom he has given her isn't easily captured.

6. Tough, Firm and Healthy

A woman who is fully equipped for her God-given tasks needs to be physically fit. She should have the necessary rest and sleep. She needs to eat the foods her body requires to give her physical strength and avoid those that detract from her health and wholeness. Her sense of well-being and self-esteem will be enhanced if she is the right weight for her bone-structure and if she is getting proper exercise each day.

God delights to speak to us about anything in our lives that we are finding a problem. He wants to make you 'tough, firm and healthy' enough to do what he has called you to do. If you have a need or difficulty in this area, ask him:

> *'If any of you ___________ ___________ , [she] should*
> *______ ______ , who gives generously to all [women]*
> *without finding fault, and it _______ ____ _________*
> *to [her].'*

(James 1:5)

7. Having Great Resources

'Having great resources' is one final definition of *strong*, according to Webster's New Collegiate Dictionary. A woman who is strong, then, has great resources. But where do these resources come from?

'The ______________________ __________ is my
______________ .'

(Habakkuk 3:19)

'The _________ is my _____________ and my ___________ ;
my heart trusts in him,. and I am helped.'

(Psalm 28:7)

'It is _______ who arms me with ______________ and
makes my way perfect.'

(Psalm 18:32)

'The _________ is my ________________ and my song.'

(Exodus 15:2)

a. Know the source

The Lord himself *has* all and *is* all the resource we need. In order
to be able to draw on that resource we must know a personal, real
relationship with God himself to be the most important thing in
our lives:

'Look to the Lord and _______ ______________ ; seek his
face always.'

(1 Chronicles 16:11)

You can't draw on his strength if you don't know him as your source.
You were made for God, to please him, to know him and to love
him. To be a woman of strength, strong in God, is first and foremost
to having a deep, personal love-relationship with him.

b. Be a good waitress

A good waitress aims to please her customers and serve them in
a way that blesses them. She is more concerned for the people she
serves than with her ability to do the job of serving.

91

'Martha was distracted by all the preparations that had to be made. She came to him and asked, "Lord, don't you care that my sister has left me to do the work by myself? Tell her to help me!" '

(Luke 10:40)

Martha was more concerned about the things she was doing for Jesus than about what Jesus most wanted from her at that moment:

' "Martha, Martha," the Lord answered, "you are worried and upset about many things, but only one thing is needed. Mary has chosen what is better, and it will not be taken away from her." '

(Luke 10:41-42)

What had Mary chosen? Just to be with Jesus, listening — not doing — at that moment. With the many demands on a woman's day it is all too easy for her to become preoccupied with 'doing things' to serve the Lord, rather than having her heart set on the Lord himself whom she is serving. But day by day and time after time, as she seeks him in what he would have her do, she will become sensitive to his voice: 'Do the dishes now and leave the beds till later.' 'Forget your list this morning and read to little Johnny instead.' 'Before you start the cleaning, come aside and listen to me. I have something I want to tell you.'

A woman who has learned to be a 'waitress' for the Lord will find her strength and confidence in God continually on the increase.

c. Wait in his presence

'Do you not know? Have you not heard? The everlasting God, the Lord, the creator of the ends of the earth does not become weary or tired . . . . He gives strength to the weary, and to him who lacks might he increases power. Though youths grow weary and tired, and vigorous young men stumble badly, yet **those who wait for the Lord will**

gain new strength; they will mount up with wings like eagles, they will run and not get tired, they will walk and not become weary.'

(Isaiah 40:28-31 NASB)

'Listen to me in silence, and let the peoples gain new strength.'

(Isaiah 41:1 NASB)

It has been said that the heated human spirit can cause more confusion than any demon. 'God, everything is going wrong today; the washing-machine has broken; please help me; show me what to do!' 'God, please keep the kids safe.' 'Lord, Mrs Smith is in such need today; please help her out.' 'Lord, our money is running out — *do* something!' God wants you to talk to him through the day and call on him when you feel weak. But panic prayers don't build a relationship from which strength comes.

God wants *you*. He wants to spend time with you, as his own daughter, but not just to hear your problems with the family, your job, the church or the people who need prayer. He doesn't want always to be talking about areas of adjustment and change in your life. He wants to tell you how much you mean to him, how much he appreciates your love.

A woman who is quiet in his presence, learning to wait before him, letting him share his heart with her and sharing her heart with him, will know resources and fulfilment far beyond anything she could possibly desire. Out of her love-relationship with God, she can't help but 'mount up with wings like eagles . . . run and not get tired . . . walk and not become weary'.

God isn't looking for perfect women, but for women who will love and honour him, women who know what it is to be silent before him. Those who spend time in his presence aren't easily disturbed, torn or worn, injured or captured. They will become 'tough, firm and healthy' for the Lord for whom they were made.

LESSON 7

The Woman of Strength

True or False

1. T F It isn't feminine or womanly for a woman to be strong.

2. T F God desires that a woman be strong enough to run her life on her own and not be dependent on others.

3. T F A woman who is strong isn't easily disturbed. This means she isn't easily made to feel unsure of her acceptability to God or of her role as a woman.

4. T F A wife who hasn't fully accepted that God requires her to meet her husband's needs and honour him first, will be easily torn by conflicting demands on her.

5. T F Nursing hurt feelings and inner wounds causes weariness.

6. T F Joy comes from living primarily to please God — not people.

7. T F The Bible teaches that women are easily deceived and therefore should not bring doctrinal teaching in the church.

8. T F A woman who is strong in God recognises and is glad that God hasn't given her the task of leading men.

9. T F A strong woman is sensitive to God and should move ahead with anything God shows her — prophecy or other gifts of the Spirit, or changes in the home — even if her husband or leaders in the church haven't yet 'seen' what she has seen.

10. T F It is important to God that a woman be physically fit for her God-given tasks.
11. T F It is possible to serve God without really bringing him pleasure.

12. T F Supernatural strength comes from being in love with Jesus.

Group Discussion

1. What are the characteristics often associated with 'strong' women that are not God-given qualities (such as independence)? Discuss why these are not godly qualities.

2. Discuss the point that a woman's strength is often undermined because she refuses to accept the role God has given her and either feels dissatisfied or takes on too much.

Personal Assignment

1. Consider how much time you spend talking to God and how much time just being with him, listening. Decide today to make building your love-relationship with Jesus your top priority.

2. Consider your other priorities. Are they in the right order, or have you subtly given one greater time-priority than you should? Examples: Are you putting the children before your husband? Or carrying out your service in the church at the expense of your job? Ask God to help you make any needed adjustment.

3. Consider the area where you feel there is the greatest need to put on strength. Share with your husband or a close Christian friend and ask them to stand with you in prayer to become strong in that area.

True or False

1.F 2.F 3.T 4.T 5.T 6.T 7.T 8.T 9.F 10.T 11.T 12.T